# The Captivating Presence

## Other Books by Albert Day:

Existence Under God
Letters of the Healing Ministry
The Cup and the Sword
An Autobiography of Prayer
Discipline and Discovery
The Faith We Live

# The Captivating Presence

by Albert Edward Day

Enthea Press ✣ Atlanta

THE CAPTIVATING PRESENCE
Copyright © 1971 by Albert Edward Day

All Rights Reserved. No part of this book may be used or reproduced in any manner without written permission, except in the case of brief quotations embodied in articles and reviews. Printed in the United States of America. Direct inquiries to: Enthea Press, 88 North Gate Station Drive #106, Marble Hill, GA 30148.

ISBN 0-89804-846-X

# Contents

| | |
|---|---|
| Foreword | 7 |
| Introduction | 10 |
| The Real Presence | 12 |
| The Splendor of the Presence | 20 |
| The Guiding Presence | 22 |
| The Healing Presence | 24 |
| The Forgiving Presence | 26 |
| The Creative Presence | 31 |
| The Supreme Experience | 33 |
| The Darkness of Apparent Absence | 37 |
| The Manifestation of the Presence | 41 |
| Life Changing Developments | 46 |
| Finding Identity | 51 |
| The Presence and Identity | 55 |
| The Beckoning Holiness | 59 |
| The Holy Presence & the Yearning Heart | 62 |
| Compassion Plus | 64 |
| Ever Widening Compassion | 68 |
| Preventive Compassion | 72 |
| Compassion and Social Action | 78 |

| | |
|---|---|
| Surprise and Splendor for All | 86 |
| Always Present | 90 |
| Otherness | 94 |
| Openness | 99 |
| Obedience | 103 |
| Oneness | 109 |
| Finally | 113 |

# FOREWORD

First published thirty years ago, *The Captivating Presence* is a powerful statement of the importance of the presence of God in one man's life.

Albert E. Day was born in 1884, and ordained a Methodist minister in 1904. His service as pastor included congregations in Canton, Ohio; Pittsburgh, Pennsylvania; Baltimore, Maryland; Pasadena, California; and Washington, D.C. In 1945, he founded the Disciplined Order of Christ, and in 1950, helped Olga Worrall begin the New Life Clinic healing services in Baltimore. Both of these organizations continue to serve today. Dr. Day died in 1973.

I grew up knowing Albert Day as my grandfather, a kindly man who made everyone he talked with feel important—a co-conspirator in living. It was not until I read this book, as an adult, that I began to understand the full nature of his relationship with

God, and his deep belief that the life of spirit needs to be made real—that it must embrace the important issues of the day through our commitment to be servants of God.

*The Captivating Presence* reveals how the practice of the presence of God can transform our lives. It shows us how we can access God's wisdom and love. Many people have found guidance, direction, and strength through this book. It has sustained them in their spiritual growth and in their daily lives.

Preaching on the Book of Isaiah, Dr. Day loved to say that we can live each day reassured and confident—we can "mount up with wings like eagles, run and not be weary, walk and not faint."

In writing this book, Albert Day hoped to inspire us to come to know and serve the strength and peace that is the Captivating Presence.

—Benjamin W. Day, Jr.

To the blessed men and women whose insights have enlightened me, whose faith has enlarged my horizons, whose loyalty has strengthened me, whose example has inspired me, whose love has been unspeakable benediction, and

To my beloved children, Ruth Lucile, Helen McKay, Dorothy, Benjamin Wilson, Mary Ellen, with their devoted mother, Emma Adelaide Reader, and

To Mary and Maurice Bowen, whose "Gently Farm" and whose gentle and gracious spirits have given lovely sanctuary to my closing ministries, the grateful pages of this limited edition are addressed and dedicated.

## Introduction

God has given me eighty-seven years in which to dream and dare and do, years of joy and sorrow, fulfillment and frustration, victory and defeat, comradeship and loneliness, love and alienation, just as your own have been.

I am eager, before passing on to a new dimension of God's purpose for me and through me, to leave with you something that may help you on your continuing journey. What He has given you, was given not for you only but through you for me, and I have been enriched by it all. So what He has given me was not for my own benefit only but for you whom I have loved. We have needed each other. We could not be what we are without each other. We shall continue to need each other even when death has drawn a veil between us. I shall carry into that other world my memories of you and what I have learned from you. If in God's wise plans there is anything I can do for you from the other side, it will be such a joy to do it.

What I want to do now is to share with you, before I depart, a bit of what has been, year in and year out, the source of whatever good has touched these years. *Stated simply, it has been an awareness of the Presence.*

## The Real Presence

There is a Real Presence that makes all the difference. What and where is it? Liturgists have insisted that it is to be found in the Eucharist. Great hymns have assured us that "God is present everywhere." Tennyson walking in the fields at eventide, waved his hand toward the crimsoned western sky and said simply, "God."   Harriet Beecher Stowe, awaking from the slumbers of the night, wrote,

>   Fairer than morning
>   Lovelier than the daylight
>   Dawns the sweet consciousness
>   I am with Thee.

Walter Carruth recalls the high yearnings of his own heart "like tides on the crescent sea beach." He comments, "Some call it longing, and others call it God." Whatever it is called it is there and convincing.

Its manifestations are varied and

unique. Mary Austin, voluminous writer, author of more than a score of books, sympathetic interpreter of the life of American Indians, unconventional religionist, persistent searcher after authentic life of the spirit, found herself one day in the Presence and at once "released from the long spiritual drought that was coincident with her commitment to organized religion." She was out with her horse, leading him over the crystal-sanded soil, pierced with the orange colored flames of spring poppies. Then all at once, "the warm pervasive sweetness of ultimate reality . . . never to go away again; never to be completely out of call . . . 'Nearer than hands or feet' . . . Only the Christian saints have made the right words for it, and to them it came after long discipline of renunciation. But to Mary it just happened. Ultimate, immaterial reality. You walk into it the way one does into those wisps of warm, scented air in hollows after the sun goes down; there you stand motionless, acquiescing,

I do not know how long. It has nothing to do with time or circumstance; no, nor morals or behaviors. It is the only true and absolute."

A child of eight or nine was playing alone near the stone cottage on the edge of a gorsey common where her family spent their holidays. This is her story, told by herself in after years. "Something...made me pause; Something...was happening...just out of sight; Something...was coming... nearer and nearer." She looked hard but could not see What was present. She listened hard but "no call nor voice came from What was coming.... I stood still for a long time. Some words which I must have heard came to me; 'God is Spirit.' So that was what Spirit meant.... I wanted to be alone for a while with the Presence which was here, and yet not to be seen. There was a big flat stone there. I did what I had never done before. I knelt down beside the stone facing the woodside. Silently the words said themselves over and over again in my mind: God is Spirit."

Looking back across the years, this woman, having become a thinker in her own right, asked, "How do I know that this event was more than a child's play and fancy? Well it has in-fluenced my life ever since." In her human relations, in her insights into the nature of reality, in her concern for the underprivileged, she was a different and better person. She had come upon something deeply significant which helped her ever after to see the true significance of the world and of human life in relation to the world.

One of the memorable confessions of that remarkable man, Dag Hammerskjold, is found in his *Markings* of Whitsunday, 1961: "I don't know who–or what–put the question. I don't know when it was put. I don't even remember answering. But at some moment I did answer Yes to Someone—or Something—and from that hour I was certain that existence is meaningful and that therefore my life in self-surrender had a goal. From that moment I have known what it means 'not to look back' and to take no thought for the morrow."

It is not only interesting but arresting to discover how often the end of hesitations begins with the arrival of a Presence. Dag Hammerskjold identifies the Presence as Someone or Something. But whatever the label, the Presence was so real and so relevant that it put the decisive question and evoked the destiny-making answer. It ended the quivering debate between the past and the threatening future.

> Asked if I have courage
> To go on to the end,
> I answer Yes
> Without a single thought.

He does go on! The going is rough.

> Tired
> And lonely
> So tired
> The heart aches...
> The fingers are numb,
> The knees tremble.
> It is now
> Now, that you must not give in...
> Weep
> If you can,
> Weep,
> But do not complain.
> The way chose you–
> And you must be thankful.

In the sense of a Presence, too sublime, too awesome, too commanding to be boxed in by the labels of logic or the dogmas of theology, there is that which ends hesitancy, gives immunity to threats, bestows a sense of being chosen for great ends, keeps alive a feeling of gratitude which inspires fidelity beyond the "call of duty."

The great prophets speak of that Presence again and again. The great leaders themselves had a sense of being led. The superb voices that still resound across the centuries humbly affirmed that they were but echoes of a Voice beyond time. *But also the common folk, who were the salt of the earth, felt that their pungency was borrowed from heaven.* The lowly certainty that met life with confidence, smiled through floods of tears, kept on keeping on while others wearied and quit, affirmed that its source and sustenance was *Another* standing by. The "great cloud of witnesses" from every clime and every country of whom the Scripture speaks, believed themselves to be just that–*witnesses* who were relating what they believed they had seen and felt and heard, something done to them and for them, a happening that had its origin elsewhere in a Presence, called by different names but operating to evoke dreams and sustain the purpose and courage to live and die by those dreams and for them.

## The Splendor of the Presence

There is nothing equal to the ministry of The Presence in its power *to keep us present to the total reality of our daily lives,* and to make our own present the story of ever enlarging insights and of heroic devotion to those insights and of decisive action in every area of life.

My own experience, I think, has something to say here, just because I am such an ordinary person who has faced the ordinary lot of man with such ordinary gifts.

I began life where daily bread was often a threatening uncertainty. The beloved grandparents who reared me would have given their very lives for me and did in fact give up much of what their latest years deserved, in order to free me to seek an education. But all of their self-denial could not summon what my growing youth required. So I learned to look elsewhere for supply. I toiled long hours for thirty-five cents and then for fifty cents and never more than one dollar and a half for a ten- hour day, at jobs that completely exhausted and finally prostrated my limited strength and left me faint upon the runway. I skimped to the very limit to make ends meet but often they did not meet. My dinner pail would be considered an affront to any day laborer in our affluent time. I was even ashamed to open it in the presence of my fellow toilers, and when I could I went off in a corner to save embarrassment. It is a long story. I tell only this much to give a clue to a host of experiences which made inevitable a belief that there is a Presence that was taking account of my plight and enabled me to endure the unendurable and to emerge with determination to veto the vetoes of poverty and reach a greater goal than neighbors believed to be my fate.

## The Guiding Presence

More than most people whose stories I have heard, I have been confronted by difficult choices. The nature of my upbringing, my limited opportunities to learn by observation what one should do in perplexing situations, the lack of confidants whose experience gave them a wisdom that comes only through experience, the social urgency, bequeathed by my ancestors, which thrust me into struggles for freedom and justice—all this over and over again brought me face to face with choices which could mean life at its best or death to all that I sought and cherished. Often at my wits end, a prayer arose from my very human dilemmas for light amid the encircling gloom. I did not ask "to see the distant scene," but only for guidance for the next step. Often, oh how often, guidance came. I could not then and cannot now account for it all on the basis of coincidence, or hints emerging from my own unconsciousness, or just good luck. I had to think of a Presence that was light and to let that light shine amid the shadows of my temporal bewilderment.

## The Healing Presence

In the fifth year of my ministry, I was stricken with tuberculosis. There were copious hemorrhages from the lungs. Sputum examinations revealed the presence of deadly germs. The medical wisdom of that day said that I must go west to the high altitudes and *stay there* if I wanted to live. I went–but with the expectations of my friends that I would return in a box. I went, but economic and ecclesiastical and domestic conditions made staying in high altitudes impossible. My mother and brother had died by the same disease. Humanly speaking, the prospects of recovery were especially dark.

After the specialist's decree, "he who runs may read," I went back to my room in tears. Death did not terrify me but it would end my labors here. I wanted to do something before death closed the books on my ministry. Not knowing any better, I knelt by my narrow boarding-house bed and said, "God, I do not ask for money or for fame but only a chance to do something before I die. Give me twenty years in which to work."

Something or Someone touched my scarred lungs, banished the dread germs, enabled me to resume my vocation in Ohio, gave me strength to carry the heavy burdens of large pastorates, to lecture at colleges and universities east and west, to finish not twenty but fifty-three years in the pulpit, and at eighty-seven continue to serve God's people amid the green fields of Virginia. I could not at any time in the past nor can I now account for it all except as the grace of a healing Presence operating in my yearning life.

## The Forgiving Presence

Like every aspiring human I have had to deal with the problem of guilt. My upbringing had created in me a morally sensitive conscience. What others could dismiss as "just one of those things" impressed me as sin. What others could let slip into the limbo of dead yesterdays, remained stubbornly in my day by day living as haunting guilt. Because of the theology of my grandparents, guilt to me was not merely a personal misery. It was "the crack of doom." It darkly shadowed my present, but what was worse, it threatened my future with an endless night in which there was no slightest gleam of hope. As I grew older came changes in my own thinking about the present and the future, but those changes left unaltered the misery of sin in memory and in immediate realization.

Happily I had heard the gospel of

forgiveness. That was good news surely. But it was only news. It was not my experience. I believed it a possibility. But *I needed to know, as one can know only when a belief becomes an event in his own selfhood.* One day the event happened. It has happened many times since.

After Gipsy Smith began his walk with God, he was counselled by a well meaning minister who was interested in this convert from gipsydom, "I hope you will not go to bed any night without asking forgiveness for any sin committed during the day." Gipsy answered swiftly, "I cannot wait till bedtime. The burden would kill me. I have to seek forgiveness hour by hour." He was not a sinner above the rest of us. He was a sinner sensitive to the moral failures that accompany every life but equally conscious of the moral renewals that may take place upon every genuine repentance.

Claire Booth Luce, in the volume *Saints For Now*, said, "The very meaning of the lives of the Saints for us lies in the fact that they were sinners like ourselves trying like ourselves to combat sin. The only difference between them and us, is that *they kept* on trying; precisely because they believed that the revision and editing of sinner-into-saint is done not by man's pen but by God's grace."

The best of us can only keep on trying. But even that depends upon some assurance that there is a grace that supplements our human effort, removing the guilt that haunts us, granting new victories after the old defeats, infusing ever more powerful aversion to sin and ever deepening longing for holiness.

That is another characteristic of the Presence, as it has been manifested in my own life. Over and over has come an experience of guilt with its misery and its distraction, its blinding of the spiritual eye and its deadening of the sensibilities and its throttling of creative powers. But in varying circumstances and with manifold demonstration, has come a vivid and cleansing sense of forgiveness. It wasn't that another human, clerical or lay, had told me that God forgives. It wasn't that I had learned to forgive myself—I *tried that and it did not work!* It was a happening with authority and with unspeakable gladness. An old hymn describes it:

> O sacred hour, O hallowed spot...
> Wherever falls my distant lot
> My heart shall linger round thee.
> 'Tis not where kindred souls abound,
> Though that were almost heaven;
> 'Tis where I first my Savior found
> And felt my sins forgiven."

John Masefield's Saul Kane cried, after his experience of forgiveness:

> O glory of the lighted mind
> How dead I'd been,
> > how dumb, how blind.

*So did I!*

Whole books are written to emphasize the paralysis of guilt and the splendor of the forgiven spirit. But neither hymn, nor poem, nor book can communicate, let alone exaggerate, the living wonder, the life value of the miracle of forgiveness.

Having been the grateful recipient of such a miracle, so often in these eighty-seven years, I cannot account for it all except by affirming that a Presence, not dependent on my moods nor baffled by the greatness of my need, has wrought a deliverance that is constantly transforming my life.

# The Creative Presence

One more fact, I dare not omit. My vocation has called for creative thinking. At first that seemed utterly beyond any gift that might ever be mine. My early efforts while in college produced pitiful five-minute essays. When I graduated and entered the ministry and took a church, I had preached only twice. The first time, I postponed my sermon by having the congregation sing a number of hymns and *repeat twice one they had already sung.* When there was no other possible deferment, I arose and began. I said all that I had to say and, looking wistfully at the church clock on the wall, discovered that I had occupied only ten minutes. I was expected to use at least a half hour. The only thing I could do was to tell what I had told them in slightly different style and then sit down in dismay. And preaching every Sunday was to be my assignment the rest of my life!

Fortunately I was given a four-point circuit as my first charge. That meant preaching in two churches one Sunday and two the next. That further meant that one sermon would last for *two* weeks! But even with that degree of sermonic leisure, I was hard put to fulfill my responsibility. Something had to happen. Someone had to come to my rescue.

The desperately needed happening did happen. The Someone did enter the picture! More than a dozen books have been given to me, by that Something or that Someone. I have been invited to lecture at many colleges and seminaries. Somehow my name is on the list of distinguished ministers who have given the Lyman Beecher Lectures at Yale. What is more astonishing is that a poll by the *Christian Century* found my name among the six leading preachers in America. I *have always felt that there must have been a mistake in the count there.* But it at least indicated that some people have been helped by the sermons which a very timid unknown was somehow helped to prepare and preach.

When I recall it all, my only conclusion has had to be that the Presence which had supplied and guided and healed and forgiven me, was at work in a divine effort to supplement my poor human labors and make the lengthened lease of years, granted me, of some consequence to His kingdom.

So again and again I have come to "the place where the trembling stopped." *Always it has been a sense of the Presence* that has accompanied the miracle, the providing Pres-ence, the guiding Presence, the healing Presence, the forgiving Presence, the creative Presence. The latest experience transcends them all. To share it is one of the purposes of this book.

# The Supreme Experience

It all began most inauspiciously. One morning I awakened to find my bed crimsoned with blood. As soon as my physician could be reached, he ordered me post-haste to the hospital twenty miles away. My own diagnosis of the symptoms was cancer. With it came the expectation of a soon end to life here.

I was not frightened at the thought of migration to another plane of life. I believed the Presence to be there as well as here. Wherever He is would be home for me, unworthy though I may be of such comradeship. On the way to the hospital I communicated my wish for a simple funeral service— two favorite hymns, "Still Still With Thee," "Jesus, Thou Joy of Loving Hearts"–the one hundred and third Psalm, the Beatitudes, a brief message of hope, and a closing prayer. I took a farewell look at my beloved hills and committed my spirit to the Father of us all.

At the hospital, five days of examination were followed by drastic surgery. Of the next week I have only snatches of memory, one of which was the face of the surgeon close to mine as he said, "we are doing the best we can for you; you must do your best too," and my reply "I will."

Sometime later came the great event. In my studies of mysticism I had read about "the dark night of the soul." But my reading had not prepared me for what befell me. Nor did I identify my agonies with the experience of the saints on the way to God. *It was night* in the sky of my soul. And it was *dark!* How dark no one can understand unless he experiences it. It was all so unexpected. When I was told of the necessity of the operation and its nature, I was fully aware of the afflictions that might be in store. But I was confident of the help of the Presence and believed that we two, the Presence and I, could endure it triumphantly.

## The Darkness of Apparent Absence

What I had not dreamed could happen, did happen. I found myself apparently alone in the darkness. That was something that I had not experienced in all the many years when the Presence had manifested itself to me. There were times in my yesterdays when my consciousness of Him was dim, times when He seemed remote, when I did not deserve a Presence, when an absence seemed more fitting. But always hitherto I felt that He was within calling distance and realized that any lack of communication was my fault, not His. Always I could look to the next hour or the next day for some manifes-tation of the Presence. Always I felt that soon or late there would be an end to the trembling and a return of the peace of a realized comradeship.

In these later years, I had practiced

the Presence as did the famed Brother Lawrence, until it seemed as real and constant as the air I breathed. It was my habit to refer matters great and small to Him. When decisions had to be made I thought of Him and asked His guidance. When people came to me for counsel, as I listened to them I also listened to Him, praying that I might, through what they said and how they said it, in the tone of their voices, in the look in their eyes, in their general manner, be given some clues to their problems. My sermon preparation always involved not only disciplined research and creative effort but "loving attention" to the Other. My daily schedule included an hour of prayer in which I came, not to petition but to attend to a wisdom not my own.

So inevitably the Presence was the central reality in my life. And then all at once there seemed to be only an absence. I was alone in my pain and bewilderment. There was no Presence. There was no light. All was mystery and misery. Years ago when preachers threatened men with hell, I had a report of a sermon in which one minister sought to make vivid to his listeners what hell might be like. He described imaginatively the moment after death when a man became conscious of himself and his situation. Everything was darkness and silence. He called aloud but there was no answer. He looked about but there was only black emptiness. Then he became aware that was to be his lot forever—alone, with himself, in darkness and silence, *forever!* Could there be anything worse?

Well, that was my plight in those terrible hours. Suffering? Yes. But I had known that before and often. But *then I* was not alone. The Presence was with me. Now where was the Presence? I found myself in company with the Psalmist in his longing for an absent God. "As panteth the hart after the water brooks, so panteth my soul after thee, O God"; "My God why hast thou forsaken me? Why art thou so far from helping me, from the words of my groaning?" "O, my God, I cry by day but thou dost not answer; by night but I find no rest." "My soul thirsts for the living God. When shall I come and appear before God? My tears have been my food day and night while men say to me continually, where is your God?"

I was not asking that my pain be less, or that I be exempted from the common lot, or that I be saved from the fate of others in the hospital whose bodies were torturing them. But I was asking for the consciousness of the Presence, for what can happen when one knows that He is there and is love. I cried aloud but apparently the only answer was the echo of my heart's wailing cry. The very memory of it is still unmitigated horror.

## THE MANIFESTATION OF THE PRESENCE

Then all at once I was made aware of the Presence. I did not *see* any image athwart the sky of my soul. Nor was there any sort of phantom appearing and disappearing unpredictably. Nor did I *hear* any semblance of a voice. But *within that darkness I became certain of a Presence.* The stillness of the night was permeated by a silence more sublime than any earthly music. More real than any seeing of the eyes was the awareness of that for which my whole being was passionately yearning. I was not alone. I was held, possessed, embraced, enthralled. I could not doubt that any more than I could doubt that it was I, who for long and lonely hours had been bereft and broken. In a moment I was healed of my loneliness and heartbreak. There were long weeks of convalescence ahead of me. But there was no more the sickness that is the death of all that is lovely and meaningful. There was only the Presence and myself, lost in wonder, love and praise. The trembling had stopped. In its place came quietness, poise, assurance, clarity, adoration.

The Presence of whom I became so vividly aware was what I had never before known. There were all the identifying qualities which had so many times before ministered to my striving humanity, in guidance and healing and forgiveness and illumination. There, too, were the qualities that at other times had made me sure that what confronted me was more than my wishful thinking, more than an entity created by my very human fancies. *What was now presented to my distraught self was The Holy One!*

If any one had asked me if I believed God to be Holy, I would quickly have answered yes. Had not our songs and sermons said as much? Had I not always prayed, "hallowed be Thy name"? Was not our communion with Him the Holy Communion? Was not His book the Holy Bible? Was not His church the holy Catholic Church? Was not His spirit the Holy Spirit?

But in the epiphany of that night of darkness and pain and near despair, *the holiness of God became an ecstasy, a captivity of adoration, a heart-smiting and heart-cleansing and heart-possessing reality.* I was caught up and then bowed in enthralled worship. I wanted to be wholly so engaged forever. I wanted everything I said or did to be an act of worship. What I had become aware of thrillingly and exclusively, was a *holiness that is wholeness!* It includes everything the human heart at its best craves, everything the human mind in its greatest moments reaches after, everything the authentic self needs for its fulfillment. It was goodness of infinite dimensions; truth transcending all limitations; beauty endlessly satisfying; mercy without limit; forgiveness equal to every desperate sin; restoration transcending every prodigality; wisdom surpassing all human knowledge; everything of value in time and eternity; and always there, without variation, for everybody, in every situation!

In the Presence thus manifested there was nothing that at any time diminishes His perfections, dilutes His redemptive powers, modifies His living eagerness to help His creatures fulfill their destiny. I was ravishingly made aware that the Presence is *always the Presence-in-the-fullness-of-His-being, in His concern for all of us, in the inexhaustibleness of His saving energies, in the responsibility He assumes for every one of His children.*

As the meaning of this holiness

began to dawn upon me, I knew not only that I am asked to be like that but *that I want to be like that more than anything else in my whole category of wants.* I knew also that not to be like that is to be an obstacle in the divine effort to make the world a good home for all His children. *I knew too that real holiness is not merely what is acceptable in any society or even in the church, but is likeness to the Presence that turned my night to day, my loneliness to a great belonging, my grief to imperishable joy.*

## Life Changing Developments

After that awesome experience with the holy Presence, there came developments of great significance.

A superlative love for God possessed my whole being. There had been a genuine love for Him for many years. His gracious forgiveness, granted over and over again, His healing of destructive illnesses that threatened my life, His guidance in the midst of frequent and frustrating perplexities, His generous supply in situations of great need, His creative stimuli awakening an oft lethargic mind, evoked not only immense gratitude but real affection. I would have been the veriest churl had I not loved Him and tried to serve Him.

But as I emerged from the dark night of trial, I discovered a new and awesome love for Him. I really lost my heart to Him. Whatever reserves there may have been in my relationship with Him were gone. I had heard people say that they were wholly surrendered to God but I always shrank inwardly as I listened. I did not doubt their sincerity but I did question their self-knowledge. How could anybody know himself well enough, his unconscious as well as his conscious self, to be sure that there were no areas withheld from God. When I have been asked, "are you fully given over to God?" I could only reply, "I hope so," or "I sincerely want to be."

But this I can say truly, "I have lost my heart to God." I am sure there must be in me much that He would wish to be different. If there is, I want it to be different too. He has no rival in my love. No thing or things, no person or persons, no power or prestige could even bid for the place He has.

My first great desire, therefore, was to run about the world and say to everyone who would listen, "Nothing matters but God." Anything else that attracts us, wins our concern, commands our time and energy, offers fun, fame, fortune, prestige, power; all the paraphernalia, the trappings, the glamour, the gaud, the glory of the world—all this is nothing in comparison with what confronted me, gave itself to me, wordlessly communicated its reality, gave birth to a new consciousness within me, opened up a new world of truth, beauty, value, and beckoned me to enter and make it my home forever!

I am not the credulous type. In fact, my best friends, who know my habits of mind, think I am unduly critical when confronted by phenomena that to them seem credible. I am wary of so-called visions. I incline to skepticism when listening to people who are always seeing things, hearing voices, taking obvious coincidence for supernatural providence. But I did encounter that which I had never imagined nor expected.

It was all sublime yet simple. It was Being, so intense that my own being was charged with its reality. It was Spirit so captivating that my spirit responded with eager gladness. It was loving beauty, loving truth, loving goodness, to which all that was less than beauty, less than truth, less than goodness cried for transformation.

It was holy in the sense that it was whole, undiluted, always itself without inner contradictions. It made me at once long to become a wholly integrated, undeviating, unambiguous person in all that is lovely, loving, lovable. It was all that to which my authentic self clings and which gave assurance will cling to me forever. It was light that will never dim, warmth that will never grow cold, mercy that will never be exhausted, comradeship that will never forsake. It was *ONE* who will always follow, always welcome, always redeem time with the resources of eternity, always be contemporary yet always a beckoning future.

This is why I wanted to say to everyone, "nothing matters but God." If one has this, and is had by this, all other things are dispensable. If one does not have this, all other things are inadequate to give life meaning and glory.

# Finding Identity

If one has this he has found true identity. Identity means who I am, what I am, what is the meaning of this life for me, what I may become, what I may do that is significant for humanity.

The unrest which is manifesting itself on college campuses, in street demonstrations, in sit-ins of one kind or another, is strong evidence that youth do not know who they are, what they really want, what is their purpose in history. They do not want to become like us, accept our way of life, adopt our institutions, seek our goals. So they are foundering and fighting in protest against what we are and the world we are bequeathing to them and, hoping in the process to stumble upon some identity which will suit them better and enable them to create a better society.

Black people are in quest for identity. They refuse our rating of them as inferiors, our assignment of them to the ghettoes, our exclusion of them from skilled trades, our putting them off with sub-standard schools, our denials of their fitness for anything resembling social equality, our frequent exile of them from our churches even.

What is even more grievous is the great number of white, literate, prosperous, powerful citizens who in spite of their prowess have not yet found satisfactory answers about their identity, who they really are and what they must become. Some are "swingers." Some are tycoons. Some are cynics. Some are conspicuous consumers who flaunt their wardrobes, their jewelry, their luxury cars, their lavish summer and winter houses. But they never find fulfillment in all of it. Some are sex-obsessed. They have made a business of bedding down with whosoever will. But they cannot answer the question, "who are you," beyond a catalogue of their nighttime conquests. They can not even say, "I am a lover," for they never have given evidence, even to themselves or their consorts, that they really know what life-giving, life-creating love is.

On every level of society and in every vocation, even in the ministry, are those who do not know what they are or what they are becoming or what they should become. They wish they were someone else, doing something else for a living, finding the fun of which they have heard but which they have never experienced, married to someone else, earning more money, giving orders instead of taking them from another whom they dislike or perhaps even envy. They feel like figures in some puppet show, with no life of their own, strung up for someone else's entertainment or profit. A writer for *Life* magazine describes herself as "a sleep walker moving through the world, unconscious of the moment's high issues." She is not the only sleepwalker loose on our streets.

Undiscovered identities or mistaken identities or misplaced identities are the basic tragedy of life. At the worst they invite despair; at the least they account for much wasted manhood and womanhood. If only men and women knew what they are meant to be, what will satisfy their deepest longings and give expression to their uniqueness and make their potential contribution to society!

## The Presence and Identity

The great gift of this latest manifestation of the captivating Presence was that it identified for me my real identity. I then knew what I want to be more than anything else in the world—a godlike person!

Do not misunderstand that. That does not mean a fanatic dream of being as omniscient or as omnipotent or as omnipresent as theology has affirmed God to be. It does mean that I now know that the identity I must seek is to be a man of godlike qualities, as far as that is possible for a limited human like myself.

And what is that? Ever since the encounter that ended my dark night, the one word which most completely suggests what God seemed to be, is the word *holy*.

What has sometimes been called holy has impressed us as a horrible irrelevance. It has been like the demure little girl's definition of a parable—"a heavenly truth without any earthly meaning." It has suggested the kind of piety whose hands of prayer are never soiled in the struggle for civic righteousness or racial justice. Rufus Jones used to tell us about the boy whose mother was distressed by his interest in mud pies. She sought to lure him away from his dominant occupation by telling him if he would only stay away from dirt, he might be an angel up in the heaven some day. His noble reply was, "I don't want to be an angel up in heaven. I want to be an angel down here in the dirt." That is what the world surely needs, angels down here in the dirt. A holiness that can exist only in the antiseptic seclusions of the monastery, or in the perfumed spotlessness of ivory towers, has little appeal to most of us. It smacks more of spiritual anemia than of saintliness.

When we say that God is holy, we

are not naming an attribute among many others such as love and mercy and wisdom and power. We are attempting to designate something that *applies to all His attributes,* something that gives them an awesome dimension. We are saying that He is the changeless One. His love never fluctuates; His mercy is inexhaustible; His wisdom cherishes all that is truly good; His power can always be trusted to act redemptively. *The supreme wonder and unrivalled glory is that He is all that He is, unchangeably.* "In Him is no variableness" is the New Testament assurance.

So we need not speculate what will be His response whenever we turn to Him, whether it be from an hour of victory or from a night of defeat; from an act of which we are proud, or from one of which we are heartily ashamed. Our heads may be held high or bent very low. We may come jubilantly to thank Him for what He has done or to barely utter a faint cry for help. It matters not who we are or where we are, a holy God is a God in whom there is nothing to adulterate or diminish or alter the transcendent qualities which our weakness or our sinfulness need. *He is always God.* Nothing is ever missing from Him if He is to be what all mankind must have to make and keep it truly human on the way to its fulfillment in Him. Sometimes the best of us have days when our dearest friend must say, "you are not yourself today." That fact gives them a hard time and sends them away de-prived of what they should have from us. BUT GOD IS ALWAYS HIMSELF.

## The Beckoning Holiness

God's holiness is unvarying sunshine for the darkest human day. It is the ceaseless music for our time of jangling discord. It is the steadfast love that woos our hostilities. It is the ever ready balm for our bleeding wounds. It is the never diminished truth that confronts us when we are hypnotized with our vain conceits. It is the unflagging good that relentlessly exposes our evils. It is the blessed patience that inspires us to "try, try again" after the most egregious failures. It is the omnipresent comfort that dries our tears and breathes hope into our dismay and enables us to take up the load we have been tempted to lay down forever.

That is a faint idea of the picture the captivating Presence evoked in my spirit on that memorable day of which I have been writing.

It is in part the reason why I want to be like God, and why it has offered me an identity that excites me and makes worthwhile every day and every task and every discipline;

If only some of that changelessness can be mine amid the changes of our human lot;

If only there can be in me that patience which reassures those who have failed to be what they want to be;

If only my enemies as well as my friends can count on my loving kindness, no matter what their momentary or persistent unlovingness may be;

If only they who need the truth about themselves and their responsibilities, may ever hear from my lips the truth even when it hurts, a truth spoken out of loyalty to them and their best interests;

If only those who need my sacrifice, even in matters in which my own dreams are at stake, may count upon it even if something has to die out of my life, or my last hope has to be slain in order to give it;

If only in moments of greatest weariness, when I am too tired to realize what another's burden may be, he nevertheless may hear from me or see in me something that will ease his load and enable him to carry on a while longer;

If only whatever of good there may be in me, may in every situation be there in action and response, in counsel and communication;

That is the human reflection of what I now see in God and what I want others to see and find in me in ready action in behalf of others. And I want that to be, not by compulsion of grim duty, but because the holiness of the Presence has captivated me.

## THE HOLY PRESENCE
## AND THE YEARNING HEART

One other very important thing happened after I emerged from my dark night in the vivid consciousness of the holiness of God's immediate Presence; I was possessed with a consuming desire to put my arm about every sufferer in the world, especially those who are dispossessed, defeated, oppressed, sick, disillusioned, impoverished, and to say, "God loves you and is here to help you and to help me help you." I had been so agonizingly alone in that darkness, that I did not want anybody to be alone in his misery anywhere.

I came to a new understanding why Jesus passed up the religious establishment of his day, the economically secure, the socially prestigious, and sought out the poor, the outcast, the sinner, the broken, the sick, the lonely. He felt, as we so often do not feel, their sorrow. He was acquainted, as we too seldom are, with their grief. On Calvary he died of a broken heart. But that heart was broken long before Black Friday, by the desolation of the common people. "In all their afflictions he was afflicted."

Most of the time we are not. We seem to have quite a different conception of life. We avoid as much as possible the unpleasant. We shun the suffering of others. We shrink from any burdens except those which life itself inescapably thrusts upon us. We seek arduously the wealth and power that will enable us to secure ourselves against the possibility of being involved with another's affliction. Lazarus sometimes makes his way to our door step. We toss him a coin and go on our way. We give our charities but we do not give ourselves. We build our charitable institutions but we do not build ourselves into other's lives.

## Compassion Plus

I am sure that some of the compassion that has been mine through the years was born out of my childhood deprivations and humiliations. One cannot hunger as I hungered, or be excluded as I was excluded, or be shamed as I was shamed by the meagerness and awkwardness of our family condition, and not thereafter have a heartache as he witnesses the similar want and neglect and misery of others.

Because in other years I have known false accusation, I have been concerned about justice for others. Because I have suffered the pangs of being asked to do what was beyond my power, I have protested against inordinate demands made upon others. Because I have known the anguish of rejection for conditions and circumstances over which I had no control, I have always stood against judgment unrelated to character or ability. Because I knew in youth the fears and the famines of a life without God, my ministry has been one of concern for the multitudes who are trying to live without God or who do not even suspect that they need God.

So inevitably I have been a crusader against poverty and war and social injustice and racism and political corruption and industrial exploitation. So too I have fostered the spirit of true evangelism.

But my experience with a captivating Presence has created in me a concern for man of greater dimension than I have ever known. Some of it came in that dark night when I faced in all its agony what it means to be without God. I thought I had experienced the limits of pain's assault in earlier trials. But this was something new and more terrible. Friends who were with me still witness to its terror. Nothing but the awful desolation of the dragging moments when the Presence I had known and depended upon, apparently vanished beyond recall, could have burned into my very being an awareness of the plight of multitudes who are living their days and nights without conscious fellowship with God. Nothing less could have made it my ceaseless concern that I may be used in some fashion to summon people to seek fellowship with Him with all their hearts.

And when the moment of deliverance came and I knew that God was right there, never to leave me, all the joys I had ever experienced seemed puny in comparison with the blessedness that encompassed my pains and my weariness. Long months of convalescence lay ahead. I still did not know what the physical outcome would be. But I did know with greater assurance than ever that God is really "all that matters."

I surely did not want a repetition of the horrible pain that had smitten my body, nor of the poverty and deprivation and humiliation of my boyhood, nor of the drab days when the conflict with tradition and custom and entrenched privilege left me in a position of desolating loneliness. But rather any or all of that than the absence of God. If one has God, he is rich beyond all computation. Hence a new and more continuous eagerness to awaken men and women to the life that is in God and with God. It now seems as inevitable and natural to include Him in conversation and to recommend Him to old friends and new, as it is for a scientist to share his discoveries in the laboratory, or for an astronaut to relate the wonders of a walk upon the moon, or for a gardener to share the beauty of a new culture in his flower bed, or for a lover to speak of the wonder of his beloved's affection.

## Ever Widening Compassion

This new excitement about God and greater passion to be identified with Him creates and sustains a concern of greater dimensions about the common lot of millions. We all have known, if we cared to know, that so many of our fellows do not meet with justice. If to be just is to be fair, to ask of no one more than he can rightly give, to grant to every one his due whether it be wages or respect, or honor, or protection, or sympathy, or opportunity, then there is much amendment in our own way of life called for.

Jesus insisted that we should surpass the crude standards set by common behavior.

Read again Matthew 5-7. Some of these patterns of human relationships seem ridiculous to our casual standards. But behind them all is the divine concern that we be concerned about our fellow men and that our concern not be content with reaction against them but seek their transformation. That will hardly be accomplished until we try to understand "how they got that way."

We do not put ourselves in the situation in which the other man has to make his decisions. We do not feel about him and his actions as we feel about ourselves and what we do. When we fail somewhere, we put the best possible construction on our own failure. We recall how hard we tried. We remember that we were not at our best—we were worn out—we had just suffered a cruel blow—we were lonely—we were suffering from traumas inflicted upon our childhood, etc. So our defense is meticulously presented by our self-interest. We therefore forgive ourselves very easily.

But let another do what we have done and we put the worst possible construction upon it. We do not take account of the effort he put into the project. We do not ask what his condition at the time may have been—maybe far from his usual best, worn out with struggle, disheartened by a series of misfortunes, still suffering from childhood traumas. Maybe this was an exception to his otherwise vigilant and heroic life. We do not offer him the sympathy we claim for ourselves. We do not forgive him as we forgive ourselves and want others to forgive us. Nor do we forget as we want others to forget something we have done or failed to do.

That certainly is not the compassion of God. "Like as a father pitieth his children, so the Lord." "He knoweth our frame. He remembereth that we are dust." His holiness is more sensitive to evil than the best among us. But it is also more sensitive to all that we are and are not—our circumstances and our wounds, our efforts and our limitations, our high moments and our low ones. He accepts even our unacceptability. His hand is always out to help us. His word to us is always a word of hope. He puts Himself in our place. He did it once unforgettably on Calvary. He is doing it all the time. If that be true, and it is, then I can identify myself with the Presence only as I seek by His grace to be and do the same. And this I want more than anything else. It is not merely a duty. It is the expression of my deepest longings. "Oh to be like Thee, blessed Redeemer."

## Preventive Compassion

There is one situation especially where this passion to be like the Presence is much needed, namely, where people are heading toward heartbreak. An assistant of mine was a most lovable fellow but he lacked sensitivity often in dealing with peo-ple. He was devoted to his work but his devotion sometimes found disturbing utterance. One night at a social gathering of the members, he really went overboard. It was evident that unless someone took him aside in compassion and helped him to see what he was doing, unconsciously but devastatingly, his effectiveness there would soon be diminished or ended. I certainly shrank from the task. How could I tell him what was wrong? It was one of those things no one likes even to mention. But finally with a lump in my throat and a prayer in my heart, I asked him to come to my study. With as much finesse as I could muster and with a genuine appreciation of his many possibilities, I let him see what he had done and was in danger of doing again. He became very angry with me. I was glad my desk was between us for I was no match for his youth and strength. The interview ended without violence. As he went out the door I was not at all sure what the aftermath might be. But the Presence was able to use my fumbling effort to help him see himself and his need to change if the possibilities of his life were to be realized. A long time after he wrote me, recalling the interview. He said, "I was so mad I wanted to hit you with my fist. But it was the best thing that ever happened in my life."

Surely compassion means assuming responsibility for doing what another needs to help him realize his potential. Most of the time it is not easy to tell another the surgical truth.

But if we quail before the pain of it, we will fail them and God and the future to which He is calling them.

The compassion of the Presence surely means appreciating others for what they are. We are not likely to open their eyes to what we prize if we close our eyes to what they hold dear. If we assume that they have no truth, they will conclude that we do not know the truth when we see it. Too often we are blind to what people really cherish in their hearts. We approach them as heathen when sometimes they are more Christian at heart than many in our church or our race or our class.

In my travels, I found myself on a train, sitting opposite a white Methodist of quick intelligence and real devotion. She was concerned about the race situation in her city. One of the things she said stamped itself indelibly on my memory: "There is a colored woman in my town who is a better woman than I am. I know God must love her more than He does me. I can go and sit in her parlor but she cannot come and sit in mine. I know that is crazy but that is the way it is, and I cannot help it." Sadly enough that is the way it is in so many American cities. And that is not only "crazy"; it is certainly the antithesis of the compassion of God!

At the root of the growing bitterness between black and white in America is great lack of compassion. We do not put ourselves in each other's shoes. We do not walk a single mile in each other's moccasins. We are browbeaten by theories of race. We are dulled by obvious differences in culture. We are living under the shadows of the master-servant relationship. We even have hidden, in our unconscious, aversions that are the result of traumas of one sort or another. A good minister in a northern city said to me, "Albert, when I meet a colored minister on the street, my intelligence tells me that he is as good a man as I am; my conscience tells me that I should shake hands with him. I usually do but when I do something turns over inside me." There is something *in both white and black* that denies intelligence and confuses conscience; something that thinks "nigger" or "whitey"; something that argues, sometimes angrily, sometimes with a show of reason, for repression on the one hand, or for revolution on the other; something that turns over inside at the expression of common courtesy or that shakes its fist openly in refusal of the possibility that a white man can be a soul-brother.

Where in all this is there the compassion to match the compassion of the Presence? Where is there any real identity with God or in God? Have we no heart for those of another race? Or for their children? Is

America a great "Melting Pot," as a previous generation boasted? Or is it a cultural furnace that destroys our humanity toward each other and leaves a charred ruin of humanity's last great hope on earth?

   I do not know what you may think about it. But since the experience of the Presence that visited unworthy me, I can do no other than try by His grace to make my life a life of godlike compassion in every relationship that falls to my lot.

## Compassion and Social Action

What will the compassion of the Presence do when social unwisdom or political injustice or economic greed lays on men tax burdens too heavy to bear, or sends 45,000 American boys off to Vietnam to die in a war that shocks many Christian consciences, or bargains away the life, liberty and opportunity of helpless thousands for political advantage?

In recalling what Jesus and the early church did or did not, it must be remembered that their situation was entirely different from ours. They had no opportunity for political action. They were members of a subject people. Their will was not consulted. Their voice was not a part of the expression of popular opinion. They had no political identity.

We live in a democracy, a government of the people, by the people, for the people. We have a vote. We have the right of protest, singly or in assembly. We help to make government what it is, by vote or by refusal to vote, by action or refusal to act. We have not only a right but a responsibility to speak and act on issues of the day. Surely as Christians that responsibility should be met with Christian concern for the people who will be helped or hindered by our use of our franchise. We should not resign from debate or decision and leave issues in the hands of politicians or generals or lobbies or vested interests of any kind. Too often they are anti-Christ in their purposes. Or at least they dismiss moral and spiritual considerations as irrelevant or impractical. No doubt some of them believe that "churchmen obviously lack the information necessary to reach a sound political judgment" and that what they themselves do is "in the best interests of the nation." *But often their judgments are proven unsound and for the very reason that they have ignored the moral and spiritual considerations which the Christian mind and heart cherish.*

Sometimes we are told "you can not make bad people good by law." The conclusion sought is that we, who are concerned about goodness, should therefore not participate in political reform movements of any kind. Few people believe that bad people can be made good by law. But we do know that bad people can be restrained from the evil they would do if there were no laws against it. We know too that people generally are protected from many assaults and injustices by the defenses set up by the forces of law and order.

It was law that ended the brutal record of company police in Pennsylvania coal regions; that abolished the inhuman twelve-hour-day, seven-day work schedule in steel mills; that restored a measure of the civil rights of which thousands of blacks had been robbed for a hundred years; that safeguarded the savings of thousands against the depredations of Saving and Loan officials; that provided bread for underprivileged masses in our fair land; that gave the right of collective bargaining to laborers who hitherto were at the mercy of amassed capital; that has been trying to make our highways safe from the speed demons that have never had a change of heart.

*Law alone is not adequate to make America the home of goodness, beauty and truth. But it is indispensable.* We are compassionate, not merely when we grant, to those with whom we have personal relations, what is due to them under God. The imminent and urgent question is "what are we doing or failing to do to the many whom we cannot touch personally but who must live and work under conditions which our decisions or lack of decisions help to prescribe?"

I may be very kind to the colored person who cleans my house or fixes my car. But what about the thousands who must live in rat-infested ghettoes, or are daily affronted by Jim Crow customs and attitudes, or are denied the right to learn skilled trades? Do I vote for legislators who will write into law what is needed to guarantee to such persons the rights we claim for ourselves? Do I ever write a letter to my representative in Congress urging action in behalf of these thousands? In my own community do I speak up when the cause of these underprivileged and dispossessed people is under discussion?

Thousands of coal miners toil day after day in peril of their lives and amid the hourly assault of coal dust with its threat of black lung and premature death. It was my privilege to appeal to Congress to remedy this inhuman situation and help save these threatened lives. Did I do anything about it?

To date forty-four thousands of American boys have lost their lives in Vietnam. More thousands have been wounded. Destruction and desolation have laid waste that unhappy land. Death has ended the lives of a half million of the native population. The debate about that war has been fierce. Many think it the sorriest adventure in which America has ever engaged. Others are sure it has been a war to save Asia and ultimately America. What did you think about it? Did you read any authentic account or appraisal of it? Did you do anything as a result? If not why not? Was that compassion?

Pete Young, in a recent article addressed to contemporary youth, wrote, "My real sins don't have to do with that liberal bugaboo called 'issues' but rather with *a certain hardness of heart.*" If we knew the real truth about ourselves in this time of confusion and conflict, we would recognize that our decisions that affect other people too often are not evidences of thoughtful concern about their welfare, their griefs, their handicaps, their frustrations. They rather are symptoms of a hardness of heart that has little in common with the Presence whose spirit is expressed in a great hymn,

> I hear my people crying
> In cot and mine and slum;
> No field or mart is silent,
> No city street is dumb;
> I see my people falling
> In darkness and despair,
> Whom shall I send to shatter
> The fetters which they bear?

Surely one who lives with the Presence must ponder and pray,

From ease and plenty save us,
From pride of place absolve
Purge us of low desire,
Lift us to high resolve;
Teach us and make us holy,
Teach us thy will and way,
Speak and behold we answer,
Command and we obey.

## Surprise and Splendor for All

This is the story—a brief glimpse of what the conscious experience of the Real Presence has been for one life:
- an emancipating assurance of the gracious forgiveness of sins;
- a revelation of available resources for desperate situations;
- a guidance in perplexities that baffle thought and research;
- a healing of illness when other helpers failed;
- a release of unguessed faculties for creative writing;
- an unveiling of the awesome holiness of God;
- a birth of a passion to be as much like God as is possible for a finite being;
- an addition of depth dimensions to compassion for all people;
- a dedication to vigorous action in behalf of the underpriveleged and the dispossessed.

Why has this story been told? Because it is a human story of what can happen to a very ordinary person when God is given a chance with him.

We are all different from each other. The difference will mean that what the Presence will be to you, will be determined by your specific need and your unique potential. God is not the Superintendent of an assembly line where the same thing is done to you on the same schedule and in the same way as to everybody else. He is not the builder of prefabricated houses which on the whole are good but do not suit the vocation or the domestic situation of everybody who seeks His help. Nor is He the clothier whose garments, however well made, will not suit the angularities of every human frame. Nor is He a general practitioner who recognizes some symptoms and whose prescriptions help some ailments but who knows not your particular affliction and whose attempted remedies will only make matters worse. God is God. He knows you better than you know yourself and if given a chance will surprise you with the aptness of His ministry to you.

The fact of our differences does not confuse or baffle the Presence. It offers Him something very precious. It makes each one of us irreplaceable. Our value is enhanced by these differences. He does not want you to be more "of the same old stuff." Nor does He want you to be *a la mode* according to the newest ideas of piety or performance. He is seeking in you an opportunity to say to the world, "behold I make all things new," and to demonstrate the fertility of His genius in the making of souls who can be exciting comrades of each other and of Him through all eternity.

This fragmentary recital of what the Presence has meant to me, as to many others greater and wiser and holier than myself, has not been to stimulate anybody to laborious effort to be like any of us. It has been to encourage everyone to recognize the Presence and to give Him a free hand in their lives. The Real Presence is the key to splendor!

## Always Present

The Presence is always present. He needs not to be summoned. He is at hand and eager to disclose Himself. Our language sometimes conceals that fact. We urge people to "seek the Lord" as if He were one of the "ten most wanted persons" in hiding somewhere. Our prayers implore Him to "come down" to us, as if He dwelt in some faraway sky. At meal time we recite, "be present at our table, Lord" as if we could set a table anywhere out of His reach.

The language means well. It intends to give voice to a need and to be an expression of humility. But to the average hearer it implies that God is distant and aloof and "hard to get." *But He is not ever!*

If there is any distance between us and Him, it is not in Him but in the vagrancy of our thoughts, the vagabondage of our emotions, the vagaries of our inattention. There is a story about a husband and wife who were celebrating their twenty-fifth wedding anniversary. They were riding along a familiar road, thinking about other days when romantic fervors assured an eager togetherness. She remarked somewhat plaintively, "we used to sit so close together when we were out riding." His laconic but significant reply was, "Well, I haven't moved." He hadn't! He was still behind the wheel as he had to be. She was the one who had moved. The space between them was her creation. She, no longer eager for pressure of his shoulder against hers, had plumped herself down just any where she happened to subside, and most of the time was closer to the opposite door than to the driver-husband.

God has not put any space between Him and us. It is we who have created whatever separation seems to exist. Our attention is elsewhere. Our affections have other objects. Our dreams are not of Him but of self- advancement. Our reliance is on schemes of our own devising. Our hopes are earth born and earth sus-tained. If we converse, it is with people like ourselves. The fabric of our selfhood has in it too little that God can appeal to.

But God is present in reality no matter what unreality our prac-tices and our ponderings imply. He is forever trying to establish com-munication; forever aware of the wrong directions we are taking and wishing to warn us; forever offer-ing solutions for the problems that baffle us; forever standing at the door of our loneliness, eager to bring us such comradeship as the most intel-ligent living mortal could not supply; forever clinging to our indifference in the hope that someday our needs, or at least our tragedies, will waken us to respond to his advances. The Real Presence is just that, real and life-transforming. Nor are the conditions for the manifestation of His splendors out of the reach of any of us! Here they are: otherness, openness, obedience, oneness.

## Otherness

If we are to become aware of the Presence, we must escape the bonds of preoccupation with self and its interests by loving attention to other realities, especially those near at hand.

Alfred Tennyson knew that, when he felt and wrote of the flower in the crannied wall.

> Little flower—but *if* I could understand
> What you are, root and all, and all in all,
> I should know what God and man is.

Of course that cannot mean that one little flower tells the whole story of God and man. It does however say that a man who can be enough interested in something other than himself, even if it be but a flower plucked out of a wall, is a step on the way to the discovery of the Great Other.

Evelyn Underhill, one of the great spirits of our time, retells the old story of Eyes and No-Eyes. *No-Eyes* takes a walk. The chief fact for him is himself and his own movement, which he accomplishes as efficiently and comfortably as he can. He ignores the caress of the wind until it threatens to blow his hat away. He trudges along steadily avoiding the muddy pools but oblivious of the light they reflect. *Eyes* takes a walk too. "For him it is a perpetual revelation of beauty and wonder. The sunlight inebriates him, the winds delight him, the very effort of the journey is a joy.... The rich world through which he moves...gives up new secrets at every step." No-Eyes lives in the ignorance of "those who keep themselves to themselves." Eyes lives in awareness of "others," other things, the otherness of nature, and is on the way to the company of those who see God.

Canon Raven, another of the seers of our time, writes to a friend, reminding him of a great passage in (the) "Pageant of Summer" in which Jeffries' "supreme exercise of his power of vision and by the magic of vivid description, makes the corner of a field come alive, so that every blade of grass or tuft of rushes strikes home as in the moments of our initiation into nature's presence chamber." Such places are "the starting place of prayer." Becoming alive to the "others" in the field, one is preparing himself to become aware of the presence of the Divine Other.

Certainly we all recall John's great declaration, "he that loveth not his brother whom he hath seen, how can he love God who he hath not seen?" The awareness of God which evokes the love of God is conditioned by the awareness of man which inspires the love of man. We are not most vividly aware of each other. We may know names, habits, behaviors, appearances of others but we are not others-minded. In "Our Town," Emily on a day's return to earth observes: "We don't have time to look at one another."..."That's all human beings are. Just blind people." And an old neighbor adds: "Now you know! That's what it was to be alive. To move about in a cloud of ignorance, to go up and down trampling on the feelings...of those about you. To be always at the mercy of one self-centered passion, or another."

That is why the simple cultivation of "otherness" is so important for one who wishes to become aware of the Presence. It may mean taking pains to become aware of things, the beauty of flowers, the charm of eventide, the majesty of a landscape, the grace of a statue, the blithe song of a bird, the scent of fresh rain, the murmur of a gentle zephyr among the leaves, the shape of a cloud overhead, the dancing dust whirling across the newly plowed field. It may mean a new attentiveness to your neighbors, their evident weariness, the sadness in their eyes, the lines of care threading their cheeks, the heaviness of their slow pace, or equally the tokens of joy, the lilt in their voices, the bubbling spontaneity of their conversation, their persistent youthfulness in spite of the calendar.

All this is the practice of otherness. It means that self has no monopoly on the attention, that consciousness is turning outward, that what is outside one's self-interest has an opportunity to enter one's awareness. The man who becomes an expert in otherness will not long remain an amateur in relation to the Divine Other. *Love is otherness.* "He that dwelleth in love dwelleth in God and God in Him."

## Openness

This takes us a step further. It is not enough to be aware of another. It is essential that we be open to him, if the possibilities of our relationship are to become a reality.

Too often prejudices have closed entrances to our minds. Traditions of family, class, sect have taken over, until there is little room for the ideas that would give the Presence operat-ing space in our spirits. What we are is the result of false notions and ignoble emotions. What we may be and ought to be will depend upon new understandings and new responses to people and events. Until we are open to them, the Presence is immobilized. Paul warns us, "do not stifle inspiration." Our stodginess, our inflexibility, our closed minds are suffocating. The Presence cannot operate within. It is as if He were nowhere around. A smothered presence is an absence.

Most of the suggestions and operations of the Presence come to us as a surprise. He sees what we do not see. He knows where safety is and where there is peril for all that we hold dear. He is sure which way lies fulfillment and where is bound to be frustration. Unless we are truly open and receptive to the surprise of His suggestions, we will never know the splendors of a life vitalized and changed by Him.

So vivid is the memory of a season when I was so enamored of my own plans that I heard from Him no remonstrance. I took what seemed to be His silence for approval. Trouble came and I charged Him with unconcern or complete absence; "why didn't you warn me? Why did you let all this happen?" Then I became aware that I had been repelled by the strangeness of the path He wanted me to take and so refused the still small voice that had tried to communicate with me. Refusing the voice, I lost the contact. I *missed His wisdom in my own fascination with the familiar.*

More and more I am learning that openness to the Presence is the only way to be present to the Presence. Two sisters, living together in a small house, were so bent upon their own plans and preferences that they drew a chalk line upon the bare floors with the understanding that each would stay on her side of the line. They kept their bargain. Each had her own way in her marked province. But both lost their way to each other's hearts. Neither knew the real presence that was under the same roof and within sight and sound of each other. They experienced only the bitterness of absence.

*If we are to know the Real Presence there must be nothing resembling a chalk line shutting Him away from any section of our lives.* He must have the freedom of the house, if we are to know the freedom which only He can bestow. There must be receptiveness to many ideas that do not fit snugly with the ideas that have long held sway in our minds. We must not live by familiar labels when we enter the polling booth or approach the altar. Shouted slogans must not be allowed to deafen us to the whispers within. We must live by the wooings of the Spirit if we are to live with the Presence. The surprising benedictions that may fall unmerited upon us are for those who are not frightened by the often surprising appeals which God makes to us.

# Obedience

Obedience is crucial if we are to remain alive to the Presence.

Jesus told a story about a father who told one of his sons to go and work in his vineyard. The son replied promptly, "I go, Sir." But he did not go. The other son, in response to the same order, made a refusal but afterward changed his mind and went. It was not the lad who approved the idea, but the one who gave it feet and hands, who kept company with his father, was present to his father in any real sense.

Here is where so many lose the sense of the Presence. There come to them hints, suggestions, directions, even inspirations about new ways of thinking or feelings, or about new relationships, or about their lives as citizens, or about their vocations. Perhaps at first they are startled, are inclined to dismiss the whole matter and to keep on just as they have always. Maybe they do give it a second thought, begin to feel it may not be so bad after all, may even develop a bit of enthusiasm over it. They may thus congratulate themselves that they are not such "bumps on the log after all." They can respond favorably to the possibility of change. There are even moments when they feel that something good is about to happen. They may even make it a matter of prayer. They realize that the Presence has been good to them and they really should be more responsive to Him. It is almost like beginning a new conversation with Him.

But the dialogue does not get very far. Other interests intervene. Other persons get into the picture. The inner glow dies down. The sense of the Presence fades. Nothing happens. Nothing is done. They have not followed the gleam. They wander in the twilight of what now *seems to be His absence but is really only their absence from Him.*

They bewail the silence that envelops them. But it is not the silence of a muted God. It is simply that by disobedience they have dulled their capacity to hear the One who has never left them. None are so deaf as they who will not hear. Disobedience is the great deafener. It is not so much the thunderclap of cataclysmic evil that does the mischief most of the time. It is the little day-by-day refusals of the Presence.

Thomas Hood, recalling his childhood when heaven seemed as near as the tree tops, lamented:

> But now 'tis little joy
> To know I'm farther
>  off from heaven
> Than when I was a boy.

Heaven had not been moved. He had moved in thought and feeling and faith. His sensitivity had become dull. Bit by bit "the eyes that see God" had been dimmed by cataracts of doubt and disobedience. Bit by bit the ears that hear the inner voice had been dimmed by wilfulness and way-wardness. God was still speaking but man had only a deaf ear to turn toward God.

It is the bit by bit that does the mischief with our sensitivities, most of the time. A shattering detonation of disaster may do great damage. But it is the steady, hour-by-hour assault of little disregard and small disobedience and tiny neglect that is pres-ent and at work upon us.

Blessed Elisabeth Elliot, of Auca fame, in her little book, *The Liberty of Obedience,* reminds us of "the difficult paths through which God may lead a soul to maturity," and of how easily we miss those paths. Often it is because *we have missed the leadings of God.* We are obsessed with a rule book, with "the letter," with our group, with the policy of our organization, with conformity to our leader, with "facile mouthing of (our) formulas."

Obedience is indispensable. *Not to a static code,* however helpful it may be at times. *But obedience to God,* who is present with us in every situation and is speaking to us all the time. Every obedience, however small (if any obedience is ever small, quickens our sensitivity to Him and our capacity to understand Him and so makes more real our sense of His Presence.

The more real our sense of His Presence, the more inevitable will be our reference to Him in every decision. "Be thou my chooser; Thou art my only choice." That cry of Dame Moore soon becomes the cry of every soul that lives in an ever deepening consciousness of the Presence. The splendors that attend His choices quicken the appetite for more of them, even as they keep Him at the center of our consciousness.

## Oneness

Otherness, openness, obedience lead naturally to oneness and are completed by it and in it. It was for this that Jesus prayed: "that they all may be one, as thou, Father, art in me and I in thee, so also may they be in us . . . I in them and thou in me, may they be perfectly one." Freed from preoccupation with self, open to what another is, responding actively to another's needs and wishes, dreams and dedications, there is realized as much oneness as is possible between two persons without in any way destroying the identity of either.

Perhaps the best illustration is in the experience of two who loved deeply:

> Every time I come to you
> And all my words have exhausted
>    Their meager utterance,

Then all I can say is
I belong to you'
And so saying I mean
That there is no thought
    in my mind
That is not saturated with you,
No longing of my heart
That has not found in you
A perfect fulfillment,
No action of my will
That is not in happy captivity
To your judgment,
No energy of my body
That is not at your service,
No moment in my musings
That does not bear your name,
No effort to help others
That is not surcharged
    and guided
By what you do constantly
In your relationships,
No stillness not permeated
With the melodies of your soul
No bit of the present
That is not involved with you

And no hope of the future
That is not prophetic
Of an eternal pilgrimage
With you under God.

    That is how oneness knows the experience of real presence, even on the human level. It is not a presence made real by sight and sound and touch but realized rather in the very essence of the selfhood as it moves through the experiences of daily life and in the meditations of the night.
*So the Real Presence is known by the humble and by the heroic and by the holy.* With the self turned outward, open to "the divinity that shapes our ends," saying "yes" and living "yes" to the Light, there come confrontation, insights, rebirths, renewals, enduements of power, *but, far better, a consciousness of a mysterious, fascinating, holy, loving One, who abides through all changes*

*of scene, all the ups and downs of existence on this planet, all the fellowships and bereavements that are the unique events of the years.*

There is in such awesome sense of oneness the assurance that came to Paul; "I am convinced that there is nothing in death or life, in the realm of spirits or superhuman powers, in the world as it is or in the world as it shall be, in the forces of the universe, in heights or depths—nothing in all creation that can separate us from the love of God in Christ Jesus our Lord!"

## Finally

Once more, thank you all for all that you mean to me, for all that God means to me because of you, for all that you have given to me in our fellowship and for the blessed hope that we shall continue to mean more and more to each other throughout God's eternity.

July 20  1971

*[signature]*

# REFERENCES
in the order cited in the text

1. *Earth Horizon,* Mary Austin, page 98. Houghton Mifflin Co., Boston.
2. *Watcher On The Hills,* Raynor Johnson, Hodder Stoughton Ltd., London, England.
3. *Markings,* Dag Hammerskjold, page 205, Alfred A. Knopf.
4. Op. cit. page 218.
5. *Saints For Now,* Claire Boothe Luce, Sheed and Ward Inc., New York.
6. "The Everlasting Mercy," John Masefield, MacMillan Co., New York.
7. *Motive,* December 1969, page 30.
8. "Flower In The Crannied Wall," Alfred Lord Tennyson.
9. *Practical Mysticism,* by Evelyn Underhill. Ariel Press.
10. *Good News of God,* Canon Raven, page 46, Harper and Brothers.

11. *Three Plays by Thornton Wilder*, pages 100 and 101, Harper and Brothers.

12. Matthew 21:28

13. *The Liberty of Obedience*, Elisabeth Elliott, pp. 59-60.

My gratitude to the above for per-

# More Presence

*The Capitvating Presence* is published by Ariel Press. Additional copies may be ordered for $15 plus $6 for shipping, or $12 apiece when ordered in quantities of 10, plus $8 for shipping per lot of 10. To order, call Ariel Press at (770) 894-4226, e-mail us at lig201@lightariel.com, or send a check or money order to Ariel Press, 88 North Gate Station Drive #106, Marble Hill, GA 30148. We accept MasterCard, VISA, Discover, and American Express, as well as PayPal. Visit our website at lightariel.com. Other titles of interest include:

Practical Mysticism
by Evelyn Underhill

Love Virtue, by Carl Japikse

Light Behind the Dogma
by Robert R. Leichtman, M.D.